3 1994 01293 1900

1/07

SANTA ANA PUBLIC LIBRARY
NEWHOPE BRANCH

D0713456

WEEKLY WR READER®
EARLY LEARNING LIBRARY

Where People **Work**

What Happens at a
Toy Factory?

J 688.72 POH
Pohl, Kathleen
What happens at a toy
    factory?

                              $19.93
NEWHOPE   31994012931900

by Kathleen Pohl

Reading consultant: Susan Nations, M.Ed., author/literacy coach/consultant in literacy development

Please visit our web site at: www.garethstevens.com
For a free color catalog describing Weekly Reader® Early Learning Library's list
of high-quality books, call 1-877-445-5824 (USA) or 1-800-387-3178 (Canada).
Weekly Reader® Early Learning Library's fax: (414) 336-0164.

Library of Congress Cataloging-in-Publication Data

Pohl, Kathleen.
    What happens at a toy factory? / by Kathleen Pohl.
      p. cm. — (Where people work)
    Includes bibliographical references and index.
    ISBN-10: 0-8368-6889-7 — ISBN-13: 978-0-8368-6889-0 (lib. bdg.)
    ISBN-10: 0-8368-6896-X — ISBN-13: 978-0-8368-6896-8 (softcover)
    1. Toys—Design and construction—Juvenile literature. I. Title.
  II. Series: Pohl, Kathleen. Where people work.
  TS2301.T7P54 2006
  688.7'2—dc22   2006012983

This edition first published in 2007 by
Weekly Reader® Early Learning Library
A Member of the WRC Media Family of Companies
330 West Olive Street, Suite 100
Milwaukee, Wisconsin 53212 USA

Copyright © 2007 by Weekly Reader® Early Learning Library

Buddy® is a registered trademark of Weekly Reader Corporation. Used under license.

Managing editor: Dorothy L. Gibbs
Art direction: Tammy West
Cover design and page layout: Scott M. Krall
Photo research: Diane Laska-Swanke

Photographs copyright © K'NEX Industries, Inc., 2006. Reprinted with permission.

Acknowledgement: The publisher thanks K'NEX Industries, Inc. and Stewart and Diana McMeeking
for their expert consulting, the use of their facilities, and their kind assistance in developing this book.

All rights reserved. No part of this book may be reproduced, stored in a retrieval system,
or transmitted in any form or by any means, electronic, mechanical, photocopying, recording,
or otherwise, without the prior written permission of the copyright holder.

Printed in the United States of America

1 2 3 4 5 6 7 8 9 10 09 08 07 06

Hi, Kids!

I'm Buddy, your Weekly Reader® pal. Have you ever visited a toy factory? I'm here to show and tell what happens inside a toy factory. So, come on. Turn the page and read along!

Look at all these toys! They are toys you can build yourself. This toy **factory** makes building sets.

First, workers think of a fun toy to build. Pictures give them good ideas. Next, a worker draws the toy on paper.

Another worker makes
a **model** of the toy.
The model shows the
toy's size and shape.

model

A building set has many plastic pieces. A **steel mold**, or form, shapes each piece. Molds are made in a place called a **tooling shop**.

steel mold

plastic pieces

11

This worker is making a piece for a building set. He puts a mold into a special machine. A steel mold is very heavy!

steel mold

Tiny bits of plastic go into the machine, too. Heat melts the plastic in the mold. The plastic shapes cool and harden. Then the machine spits them out.

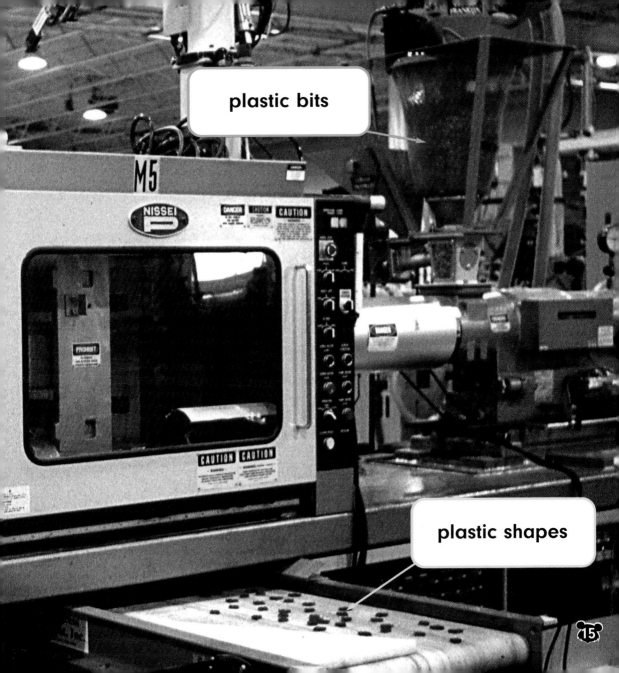

plastic bits

plastic shapes

Each building set needs directions. A worker makes them up on a computer. The directions tell how to build the toy.

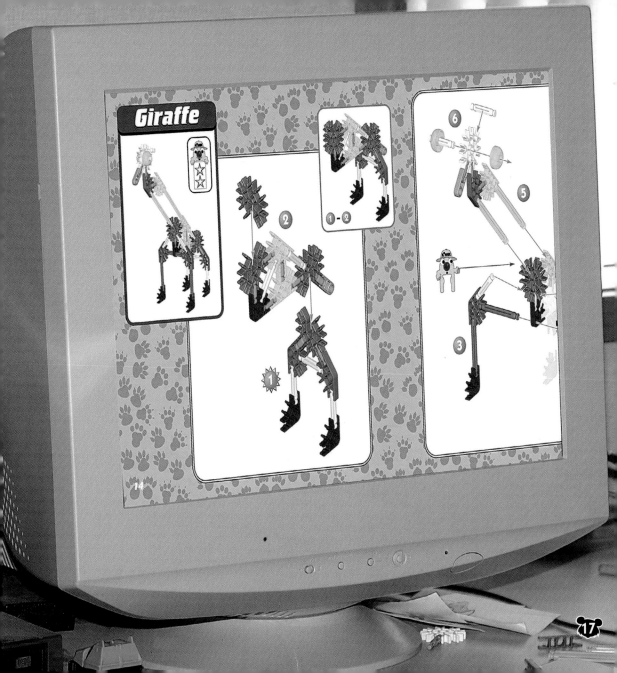

Kids come to test the building set. They follow the directions to build the toy. They help make sure the building set works.

Each building set comes packed in a box. Wow! Look at this set! It is ready to take home and build.

🐻 Glossary

directions — words and pictures that tell how to do something or make something

factory — a place where many machines and workers make things

model — a sample of a new toy or some other object that shows what it will look like

mold — a hollow form that keeps hot liquid in a certain shape until it cools and becomes hard

steel — a hard, strong metal made of iron

tooling shop — a place where workers make steel molds and other parts for machines

🐻 For More Information

Books

Fire Truck Factory. Catherine Anderson (Heinemann)

Teddy Bears from Start to Finish. Made in the USA (series). Tanya Lee Stone (Blackbirch Press)

Web Sites

How Everyday Things Are Made
manufacturing.stanford.edu
Enjoy some fun video tours of factories.

K'NEX
www.knex.com
See models you can build and play games at Club K'NEX.

Publisher's note to educators and parents: Our editors have carefully reviewed these Web sites to ensure that they are suitable for children. Many Web sites change frequently, however, and we cannot guarantee that a site's future contents will continue to meet our high standards of quality and educational value. Be advised that children should be closely supervised whenever they access the Internet.

 # Index

About the Author

Kathleen Pohl has written and edited many children's books. Among them are animal tales, rhyming books, retold classics, and the forty-book series *Nature Close-Ups*. She also served for many years as top editor of *Taste of Home* and *Country Woman* magazines. She and her husband, Bruce, live among beautiful Wisconsin woods and share their home with six goats, a llama, and all kinds of wonderful woodland creatures.